to the version of myself I haven't met yet

2024

A book for those who would know Death

Picture Writer at Work.....

it was a complete wilderness,

and in cases of peril and danger

the most peaceable and prosperous

knew no higher power to appeal to

than the revolver and bowie knife.

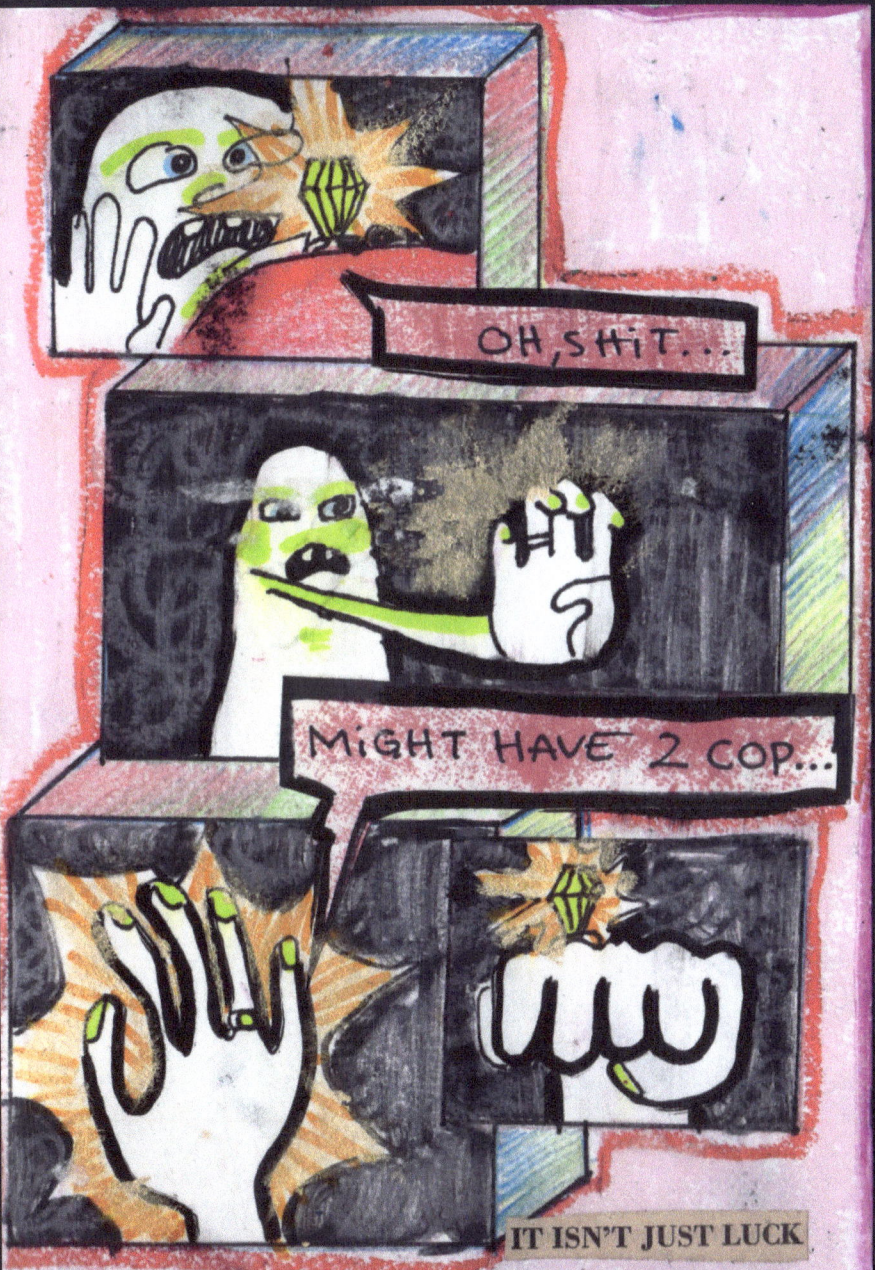

She had a million dollars,
She also had a past

SHE GOT LOST...

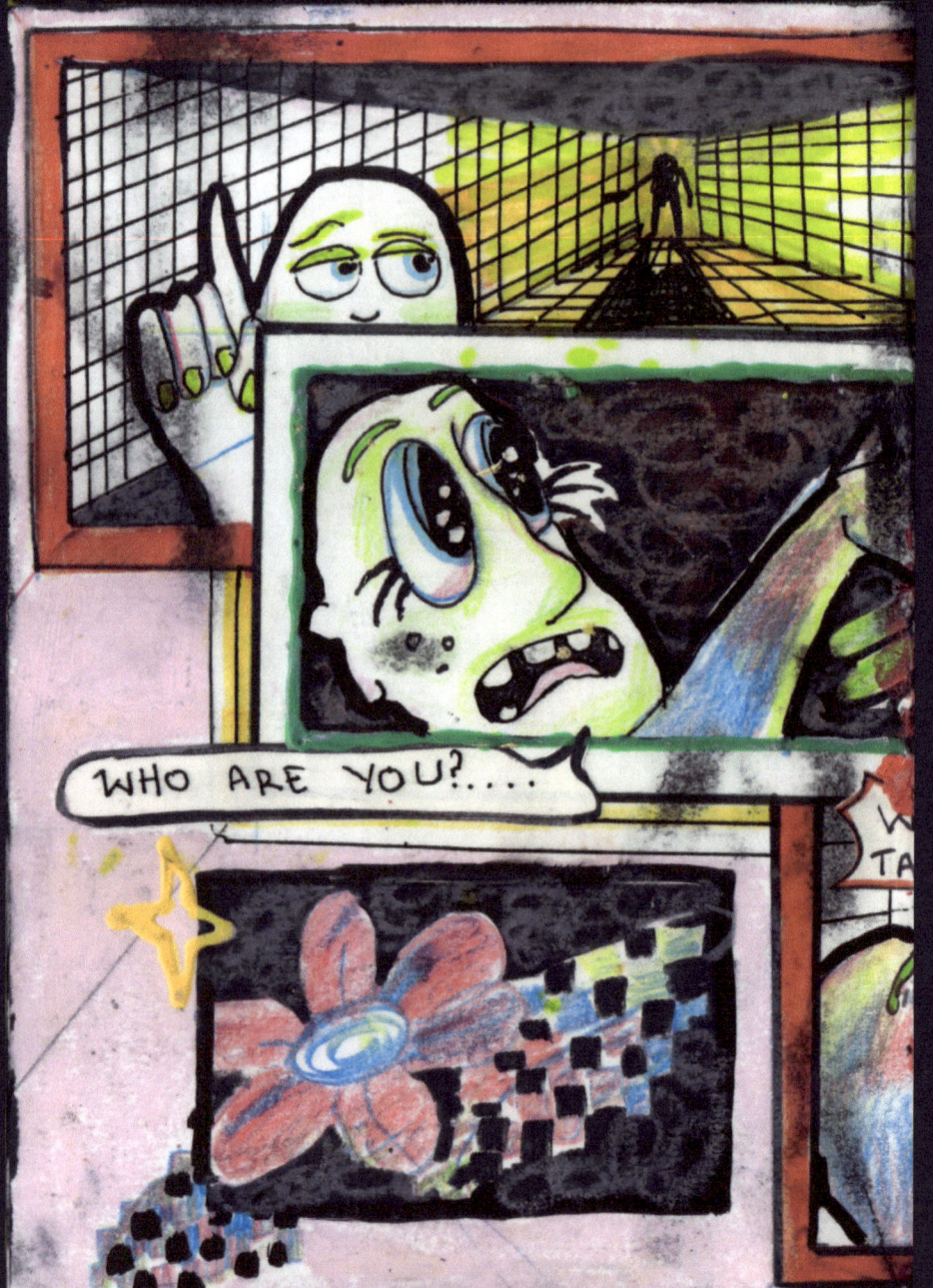

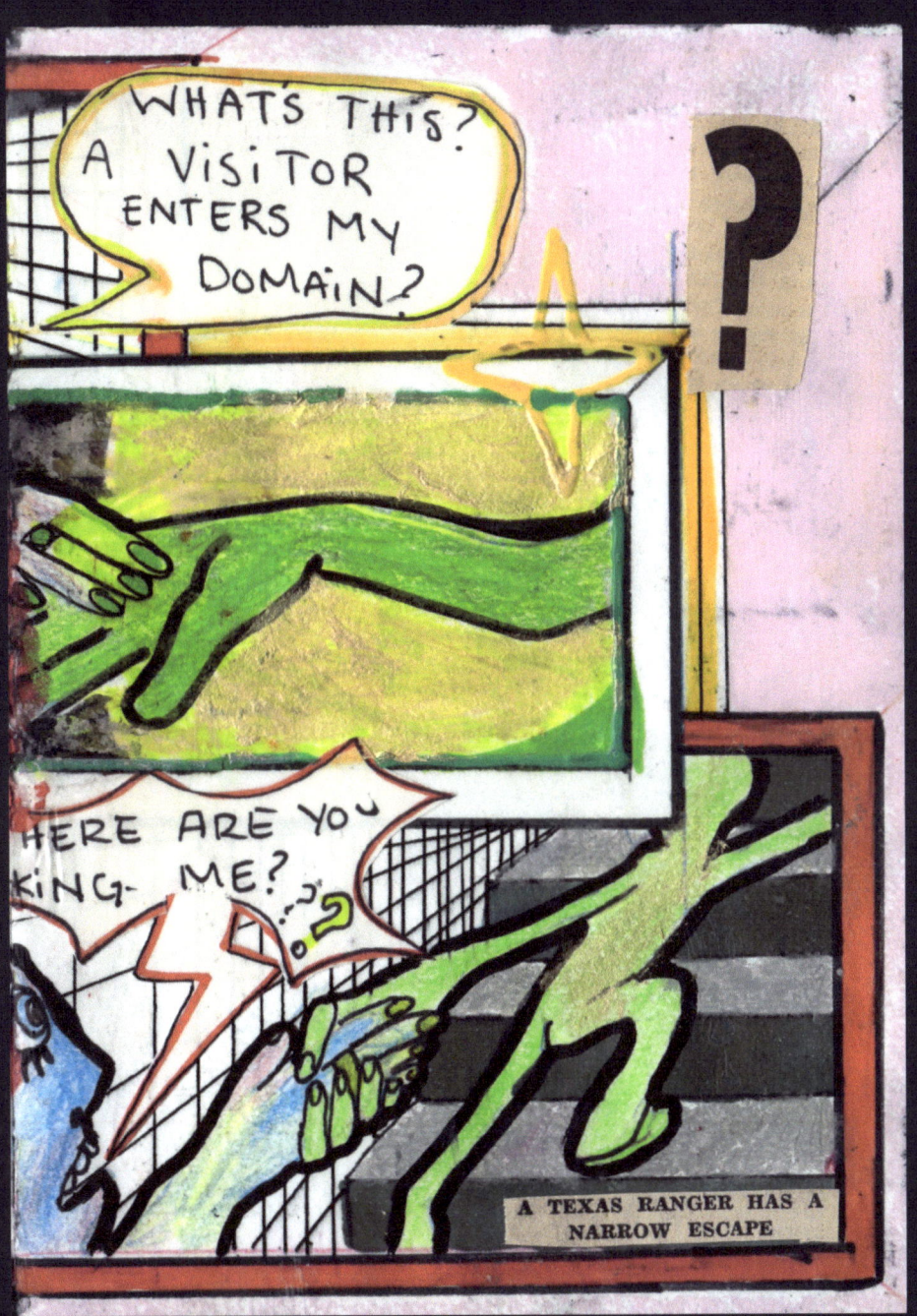

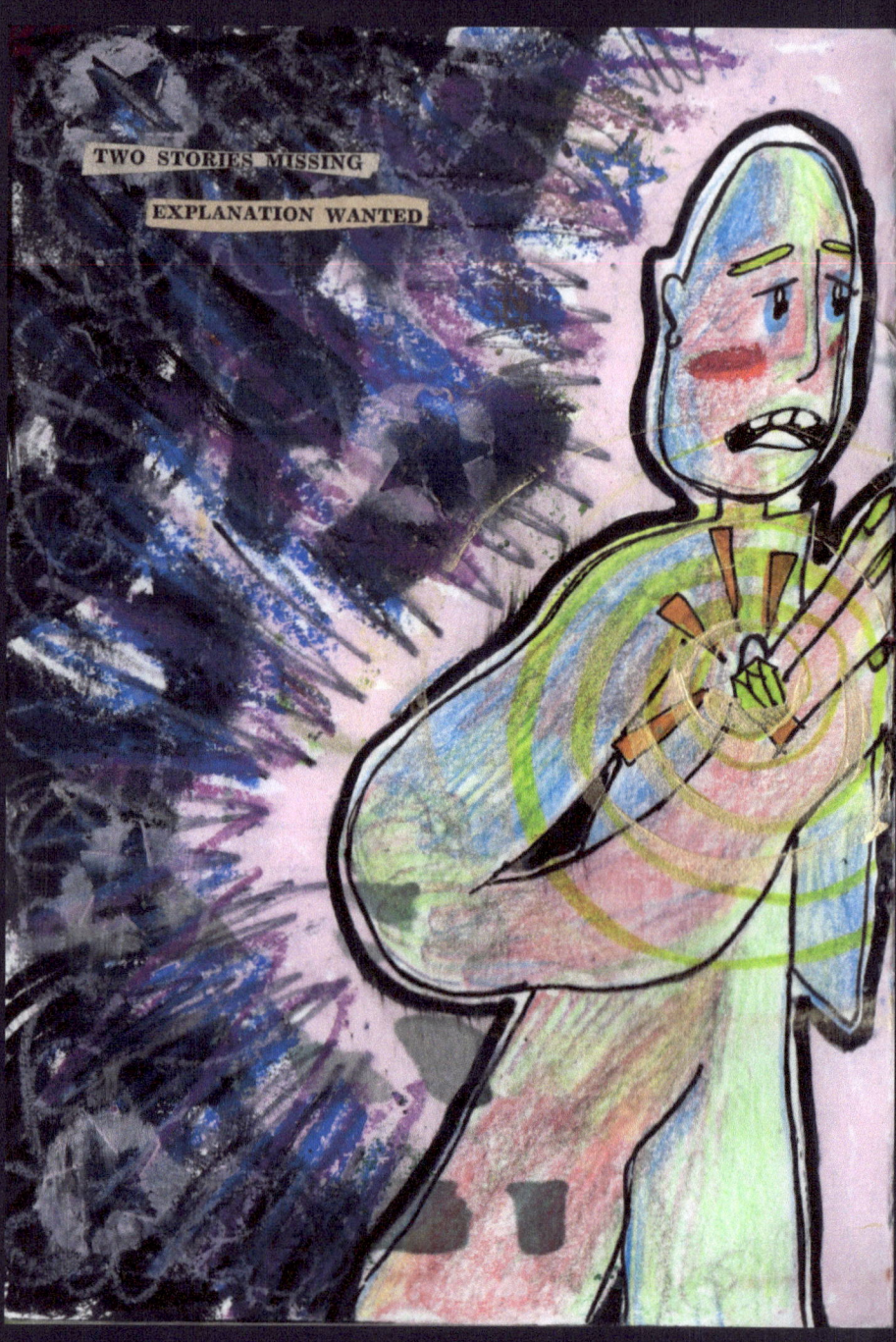

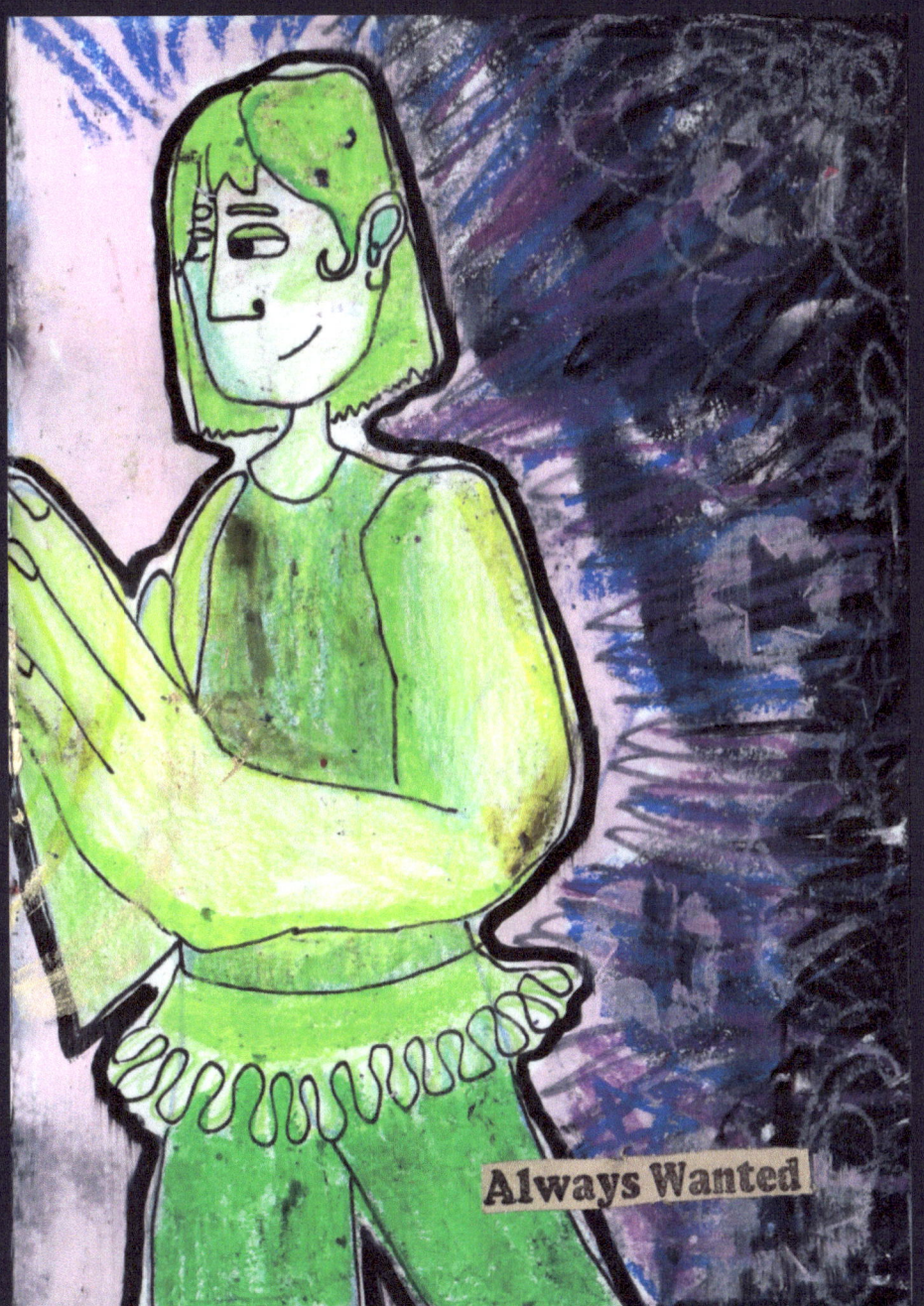

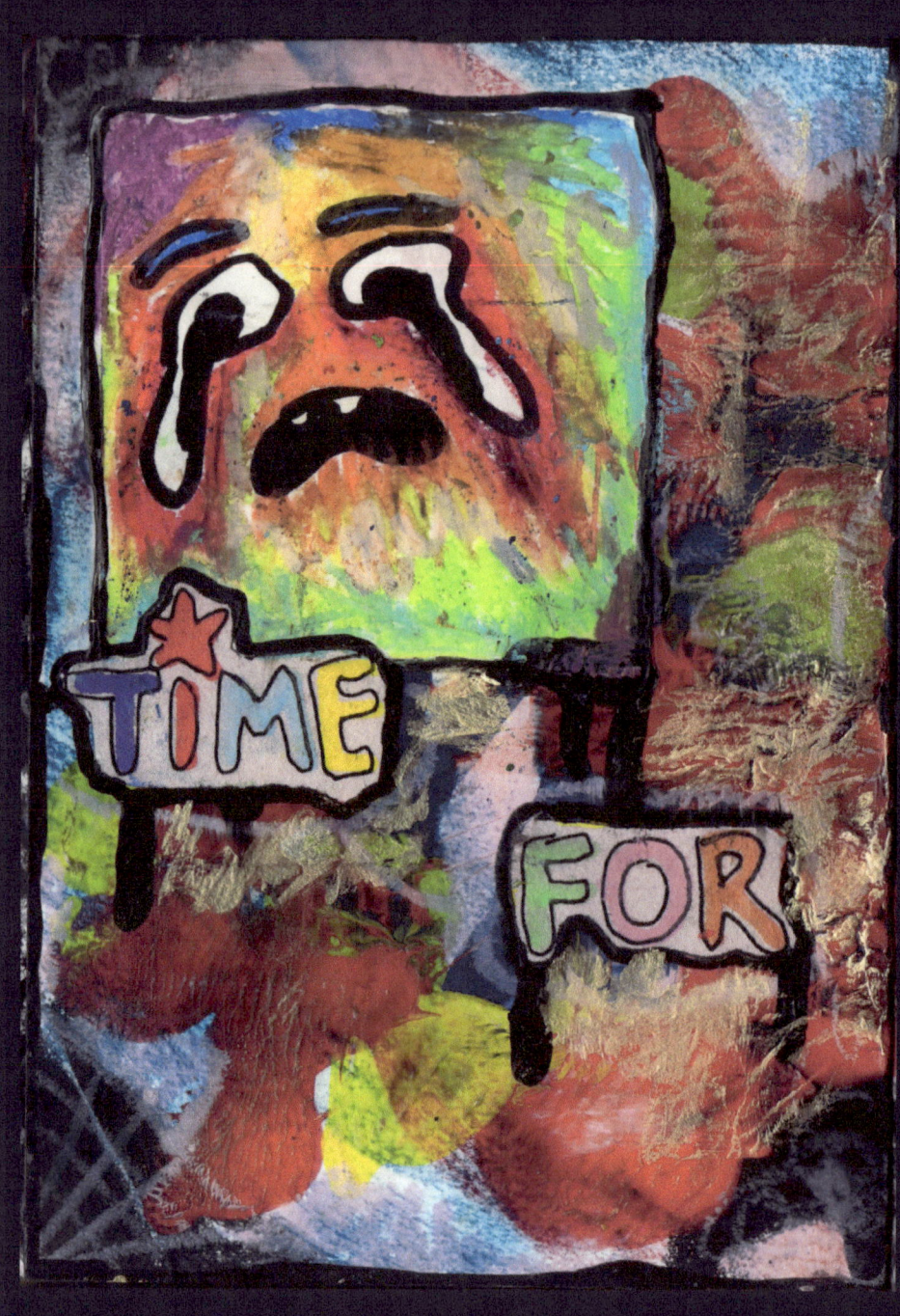

COSMIC

FOUND IN THE

THE FALL OF THE

Modern

Dependable Drugs

SUFFERING!

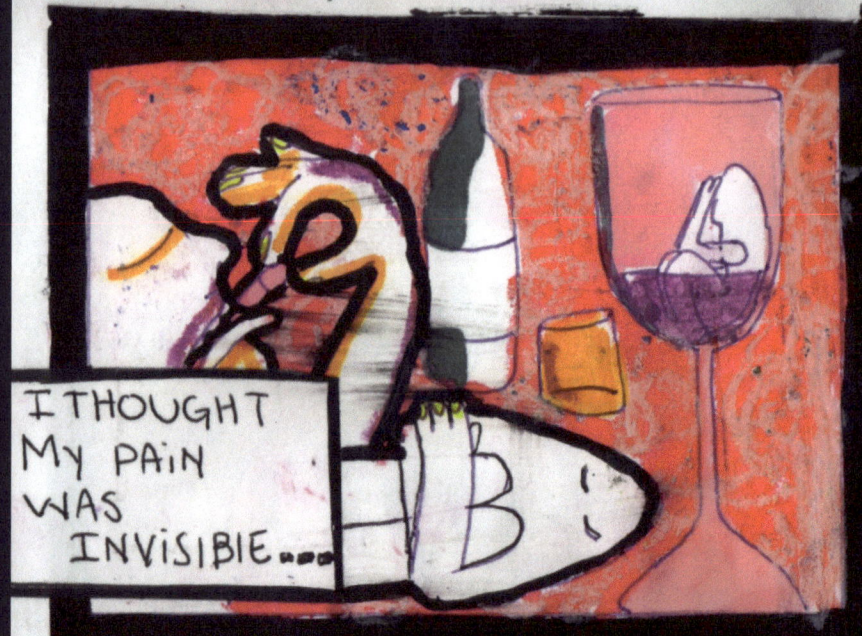
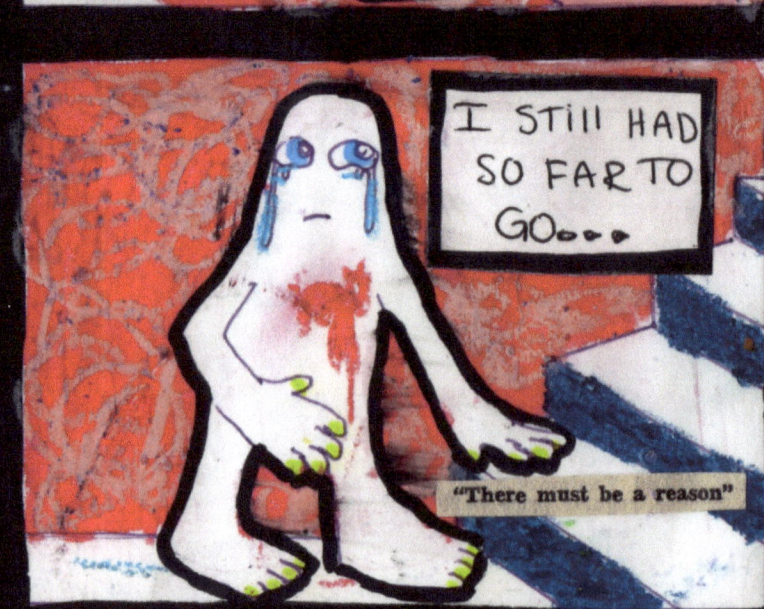

UP, UP, UP, NEVERENDING STEPS TO INFINITY

BUT I GOT TIRED OF RUNNING.

I HAD TO TURN & FACE THE THINGS I WAS RUNNING FROM.

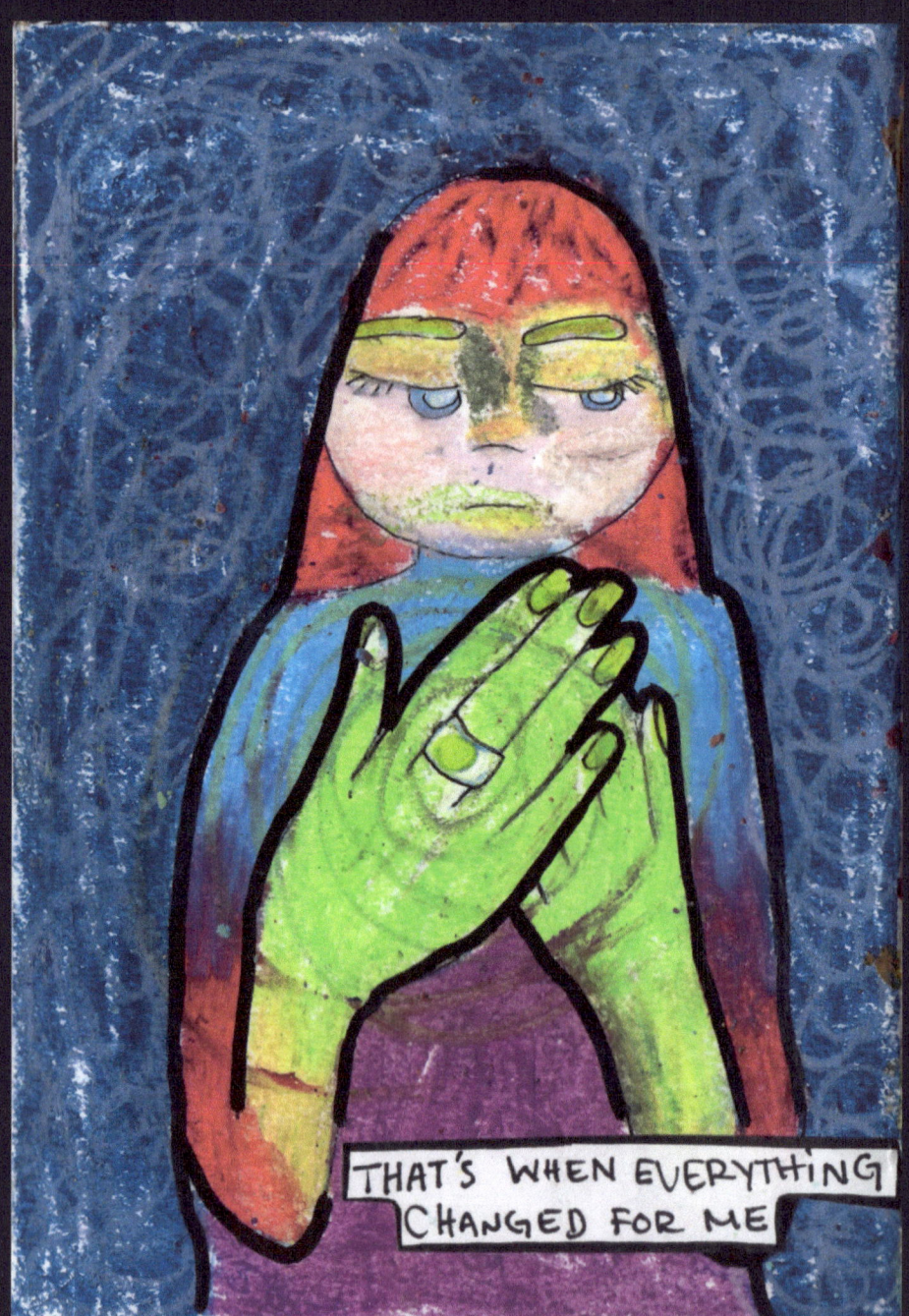

THIS HOLE IS SHAPED LIKE ME.

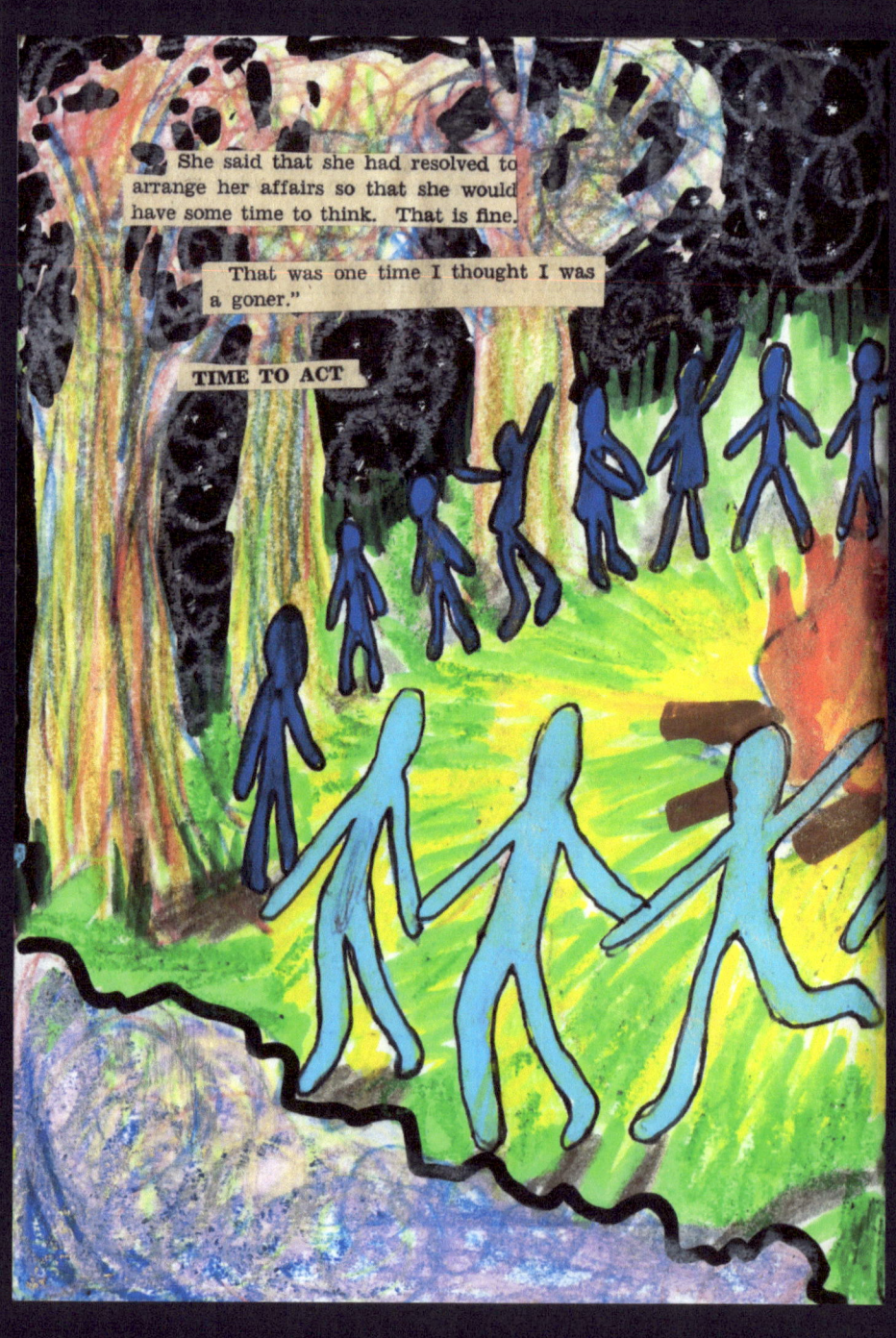

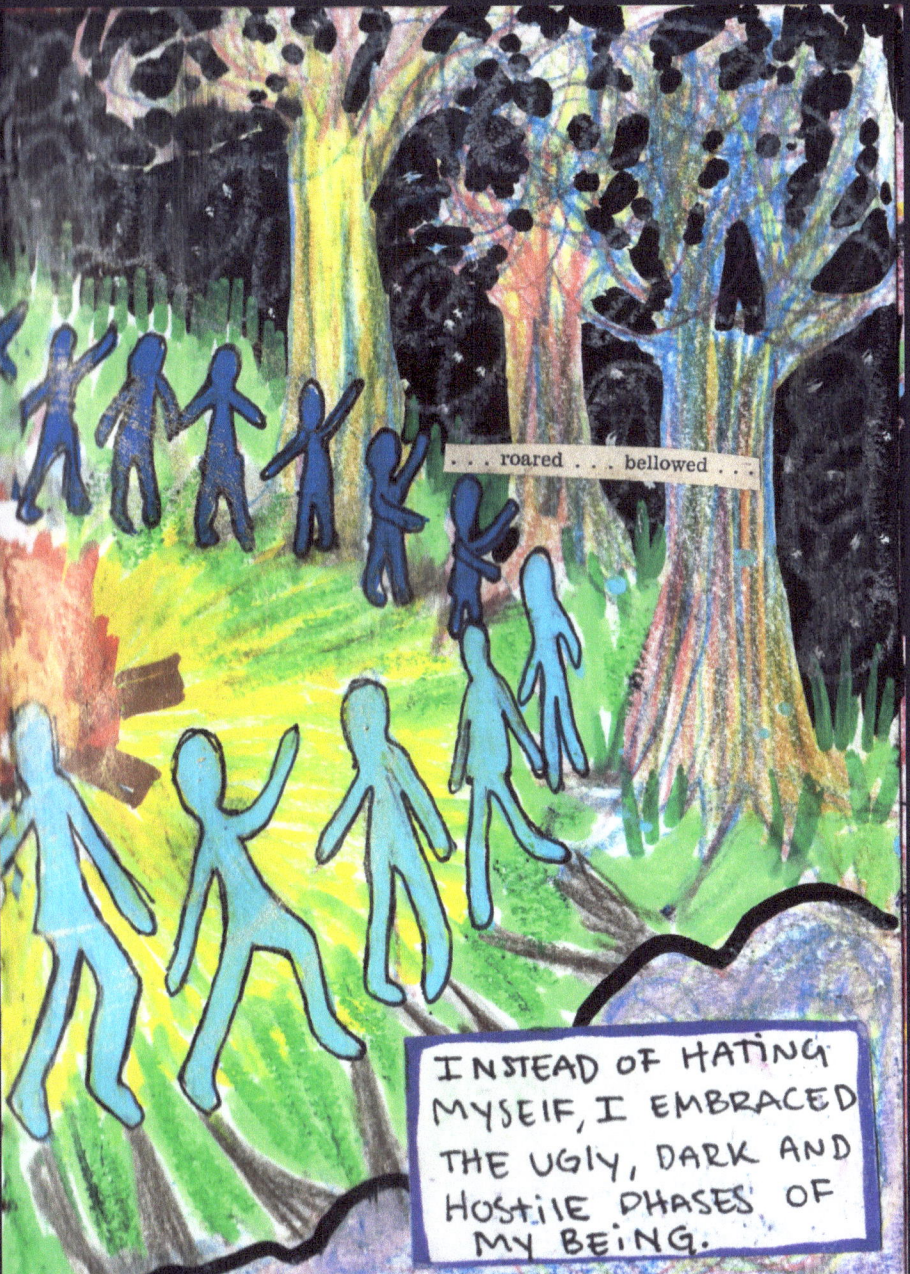

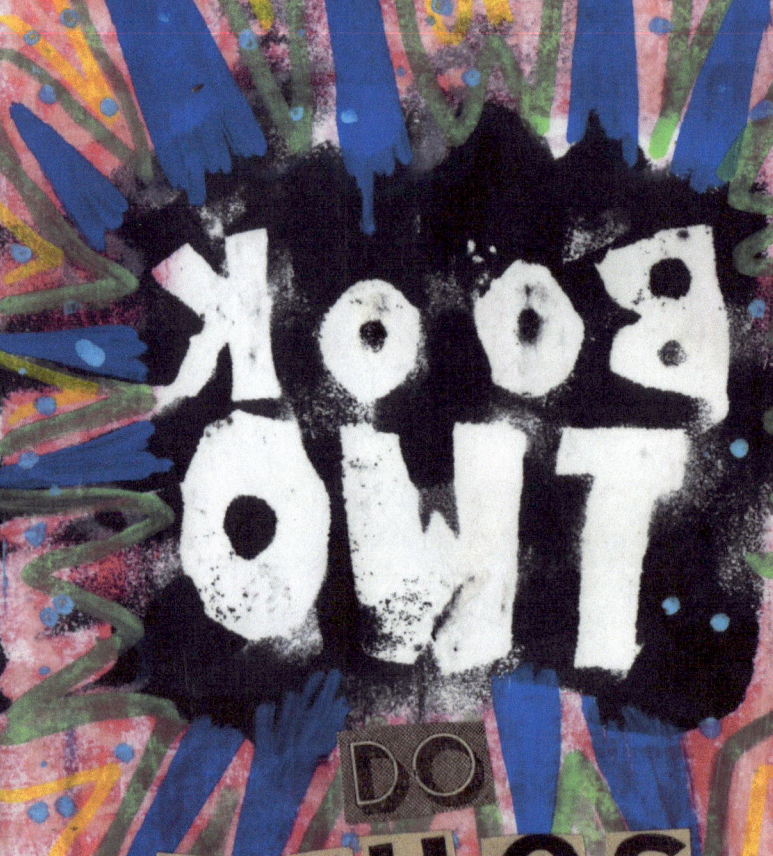

BOOK TWO

build your home

IN THESE HILLS

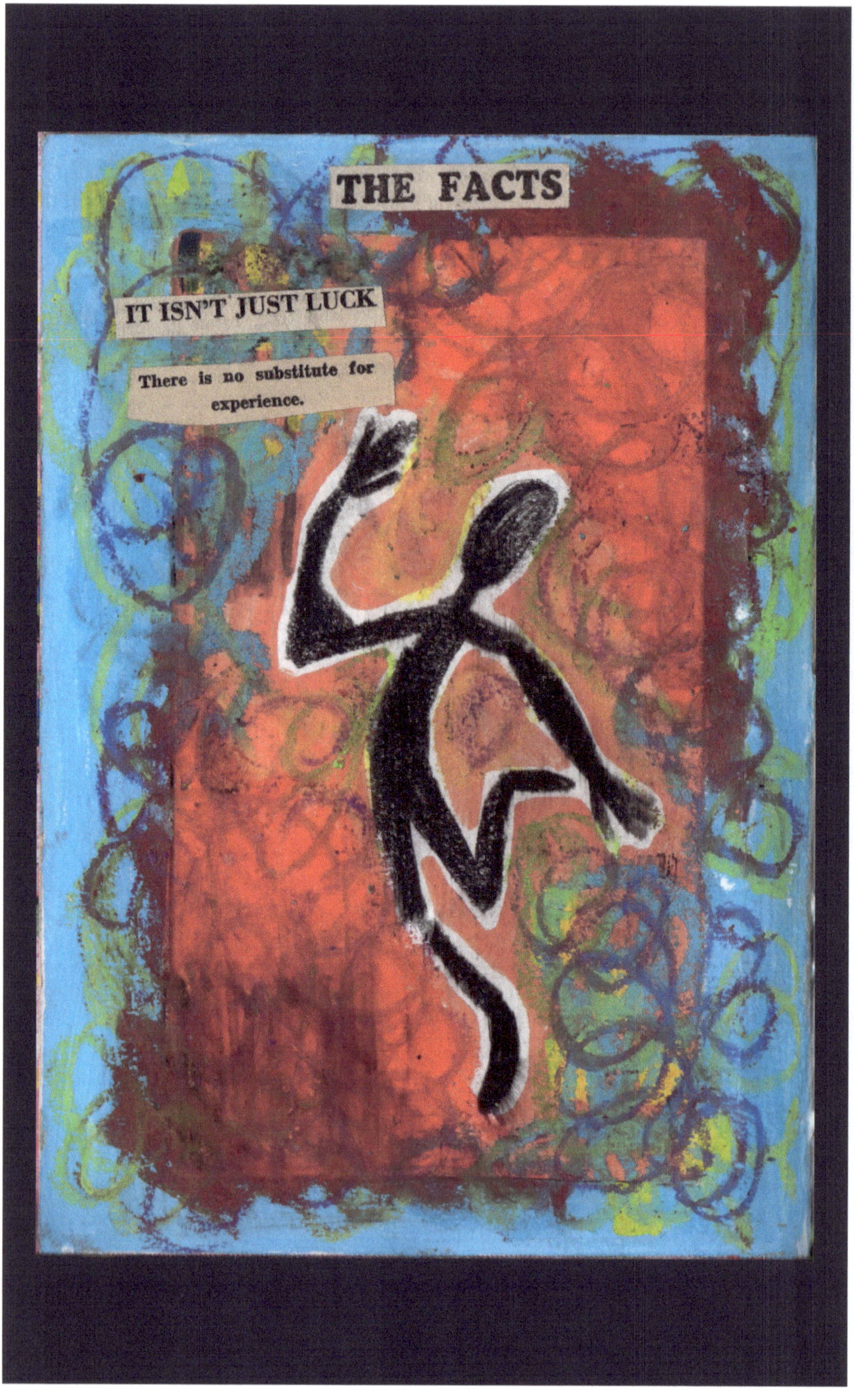

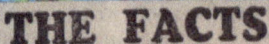

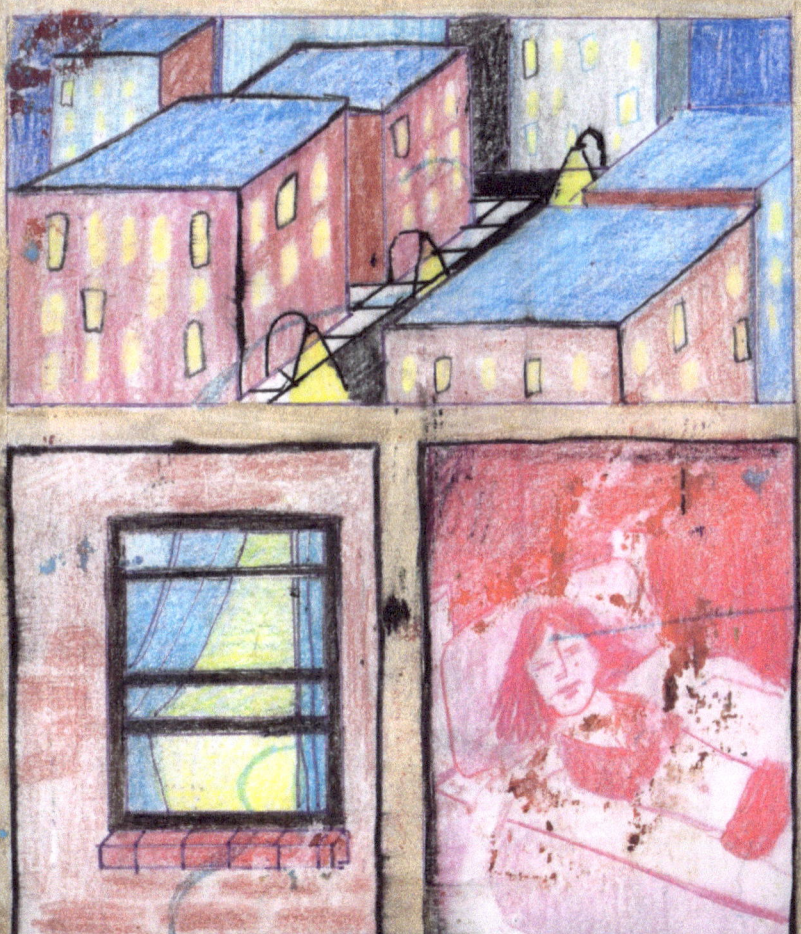

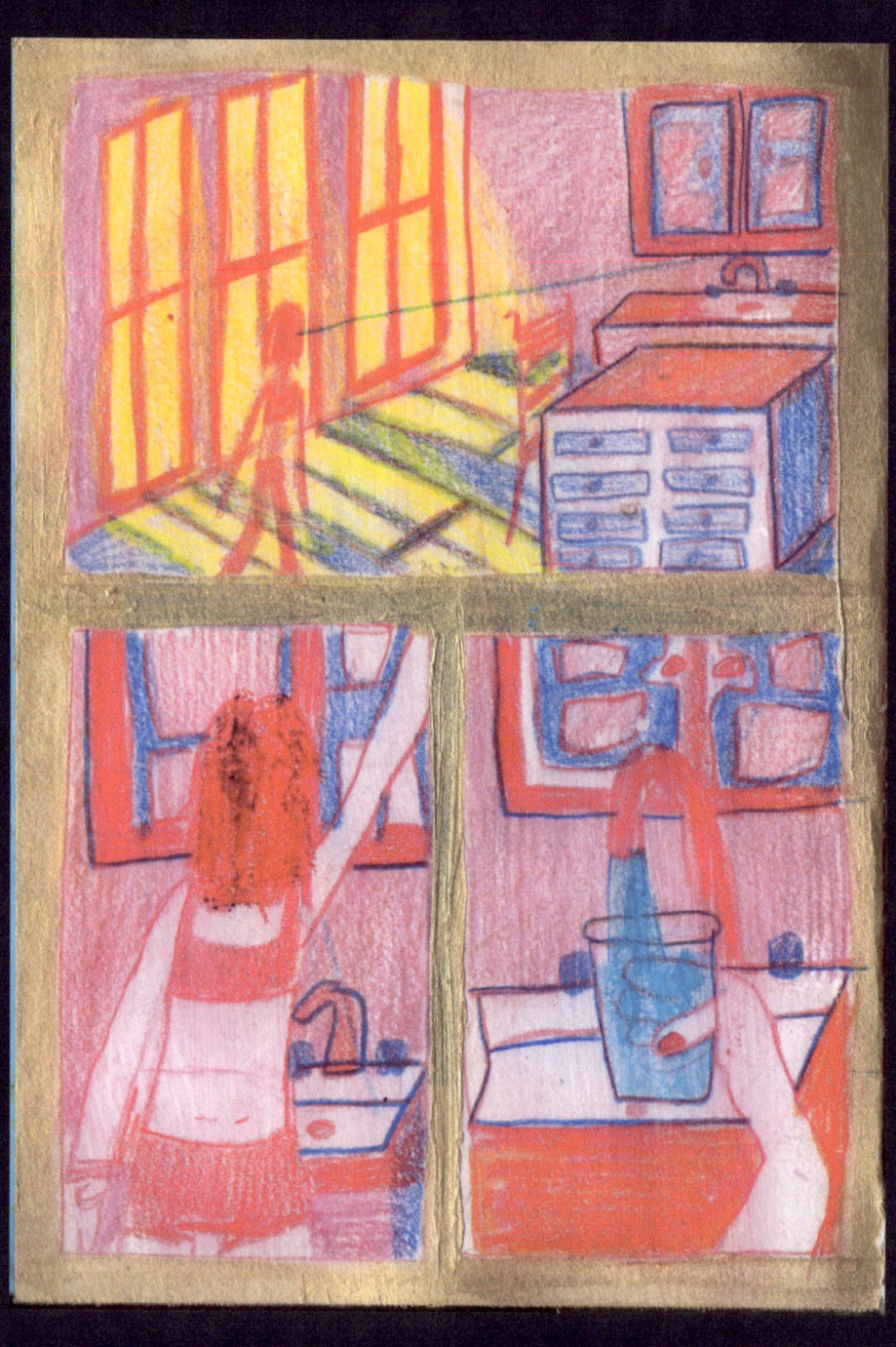

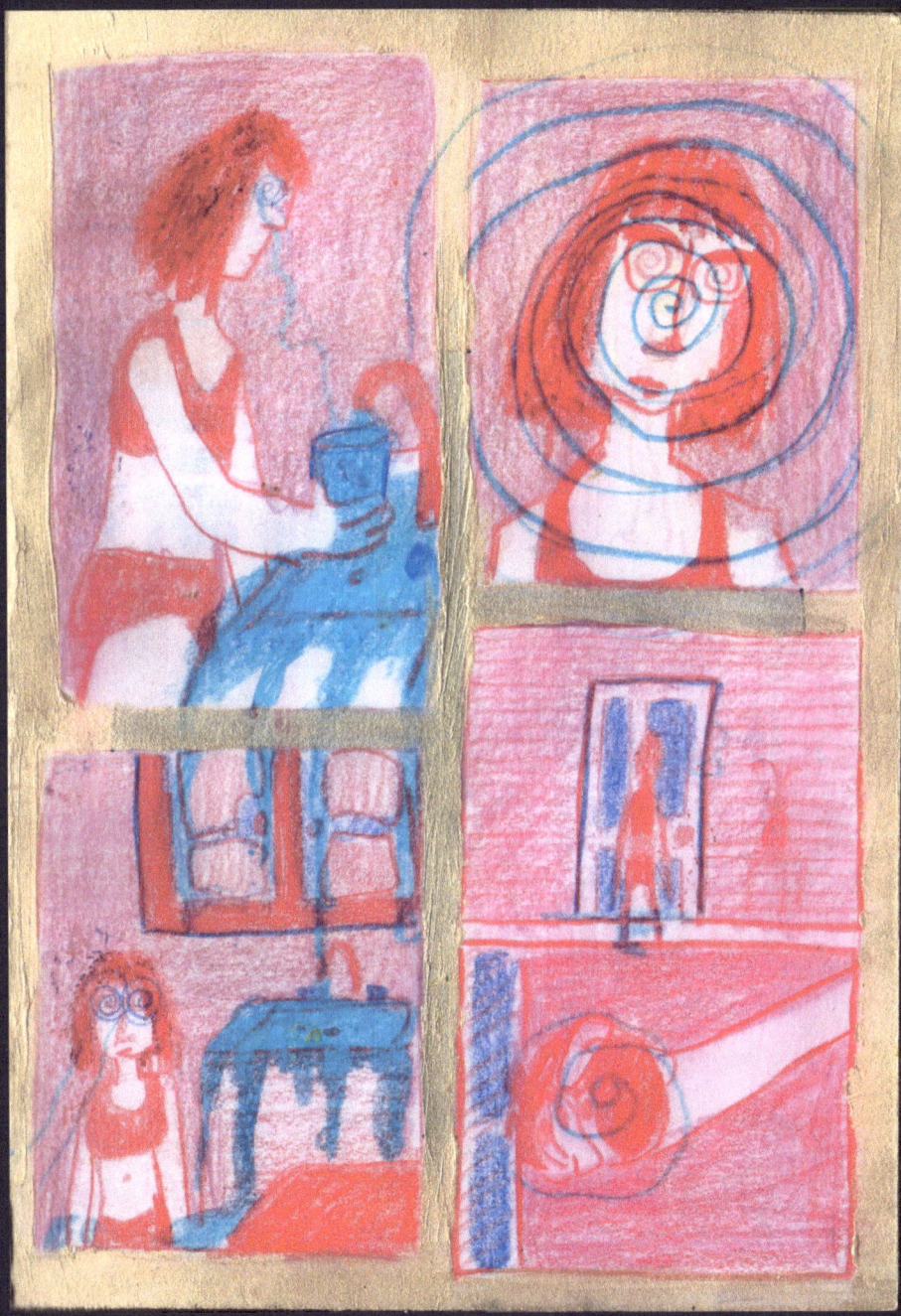

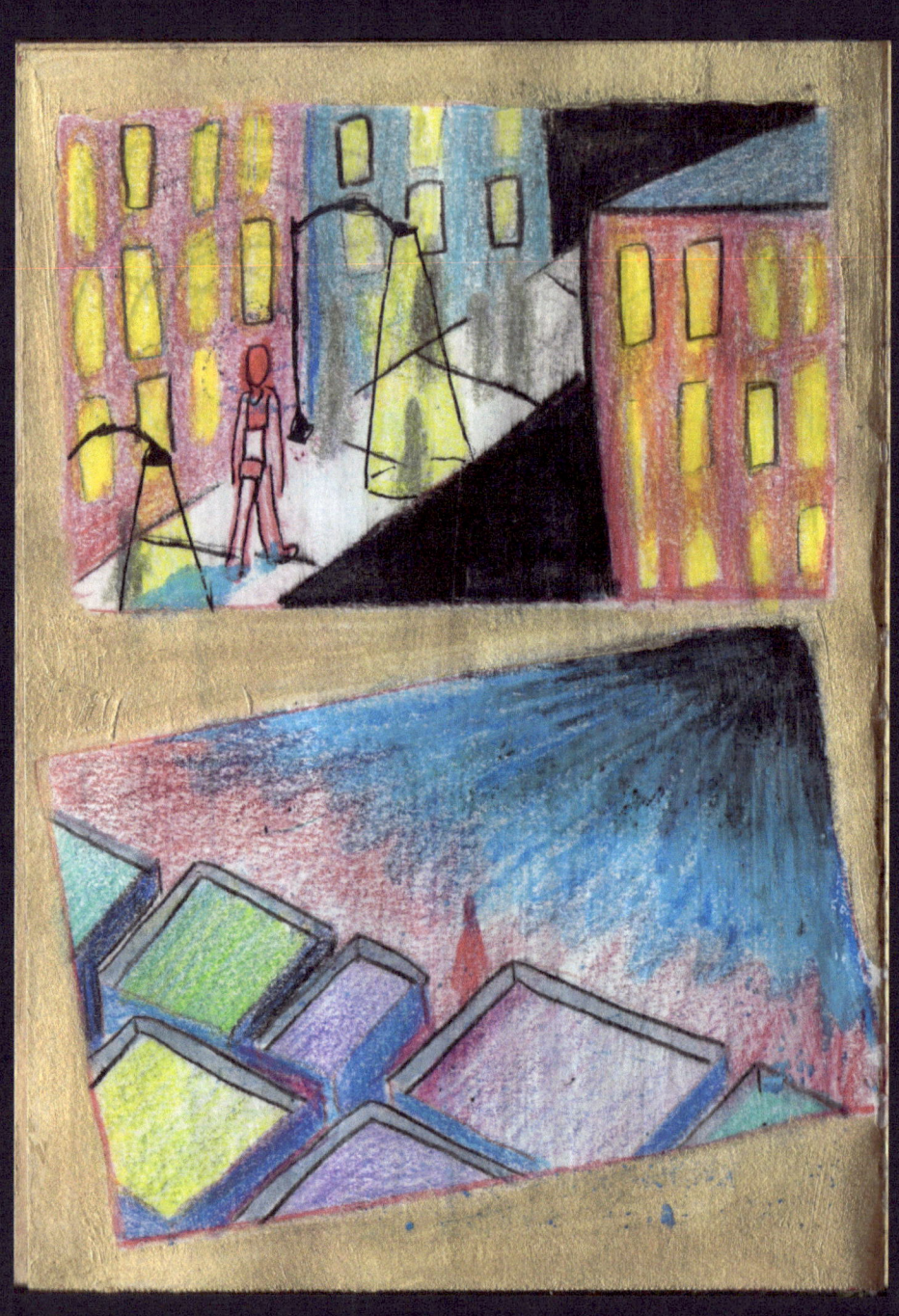

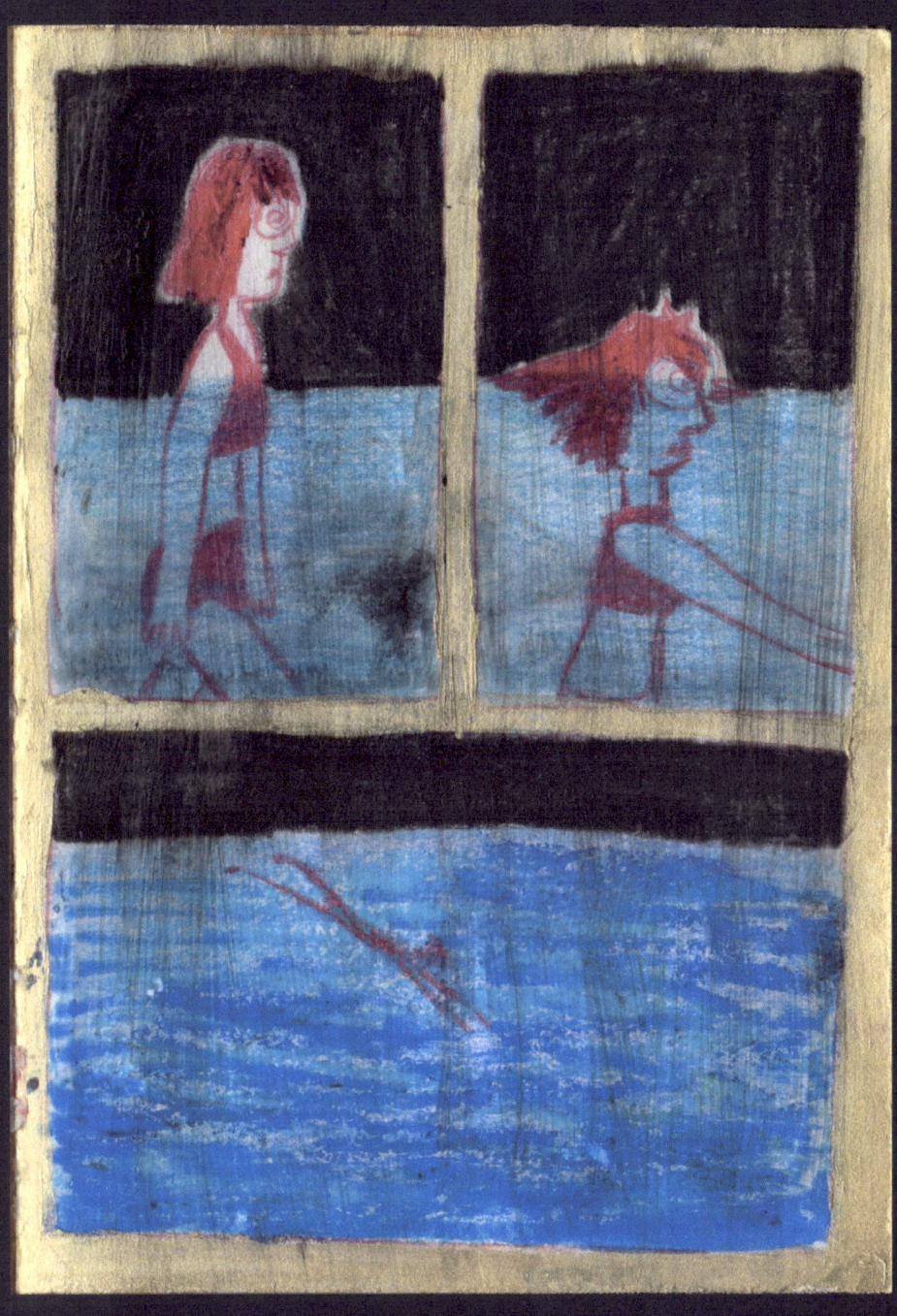

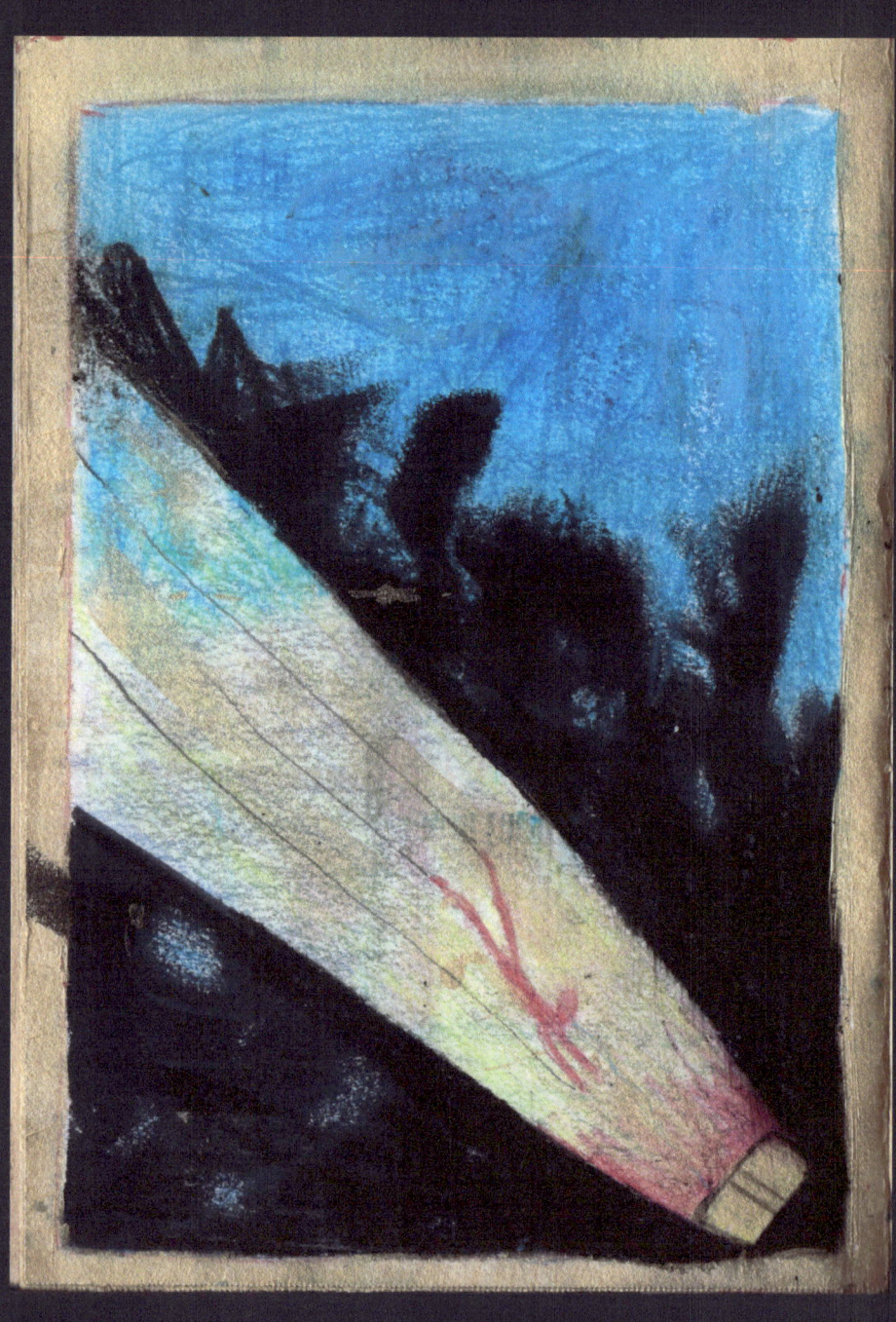

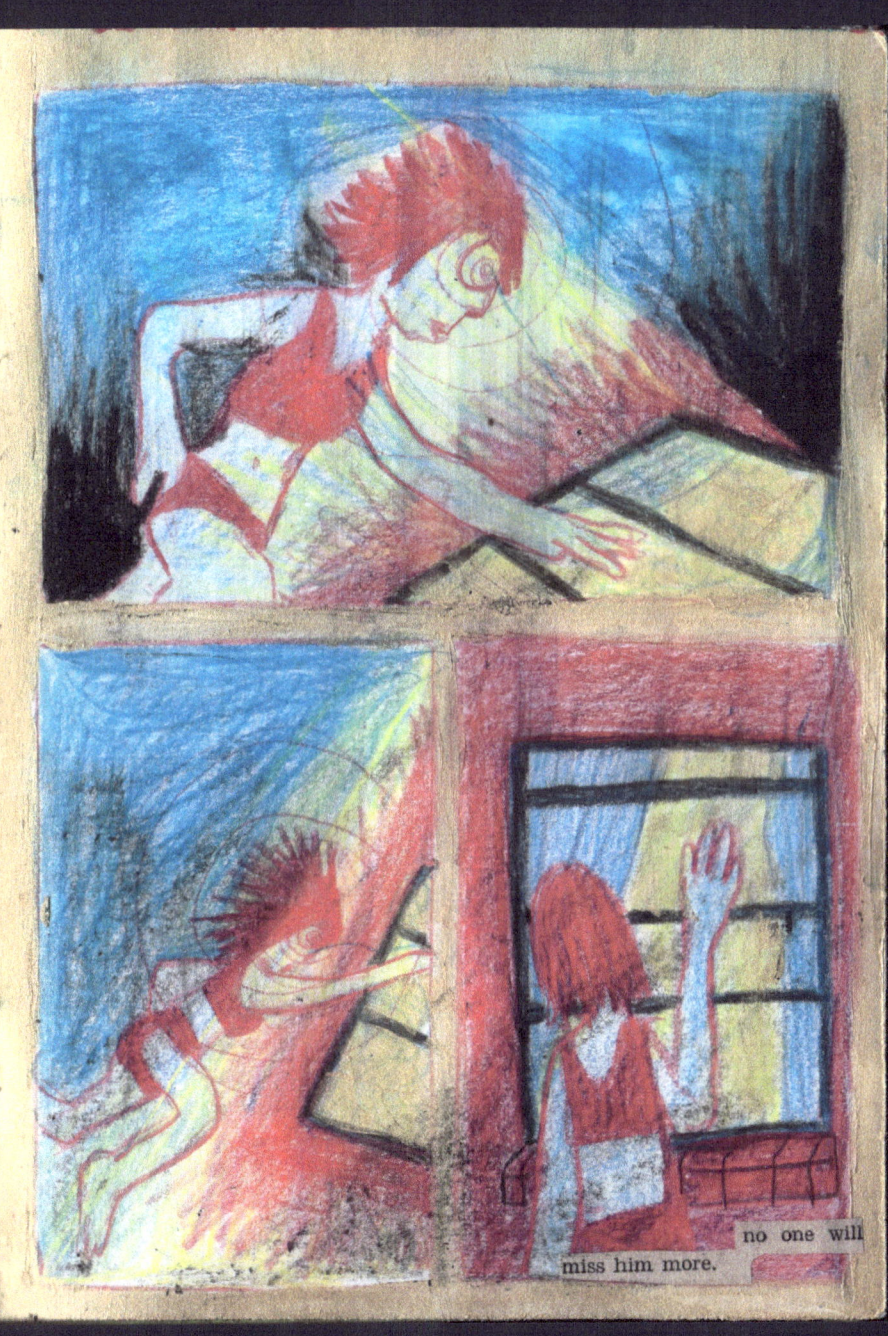

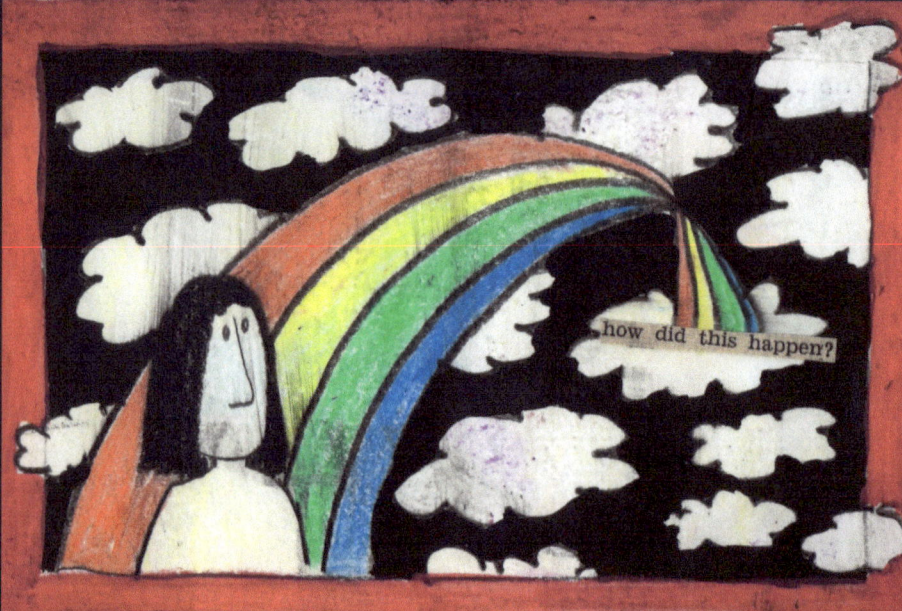
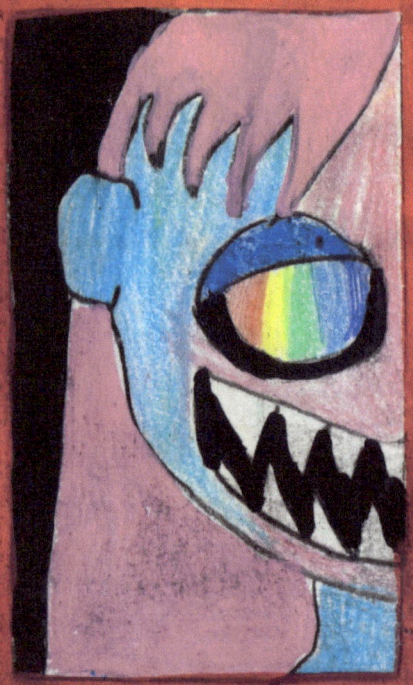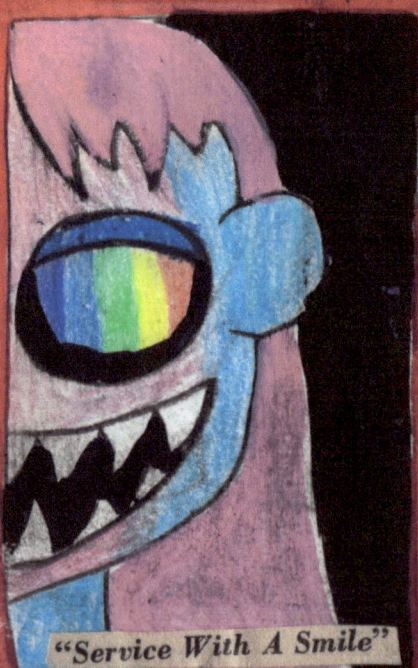

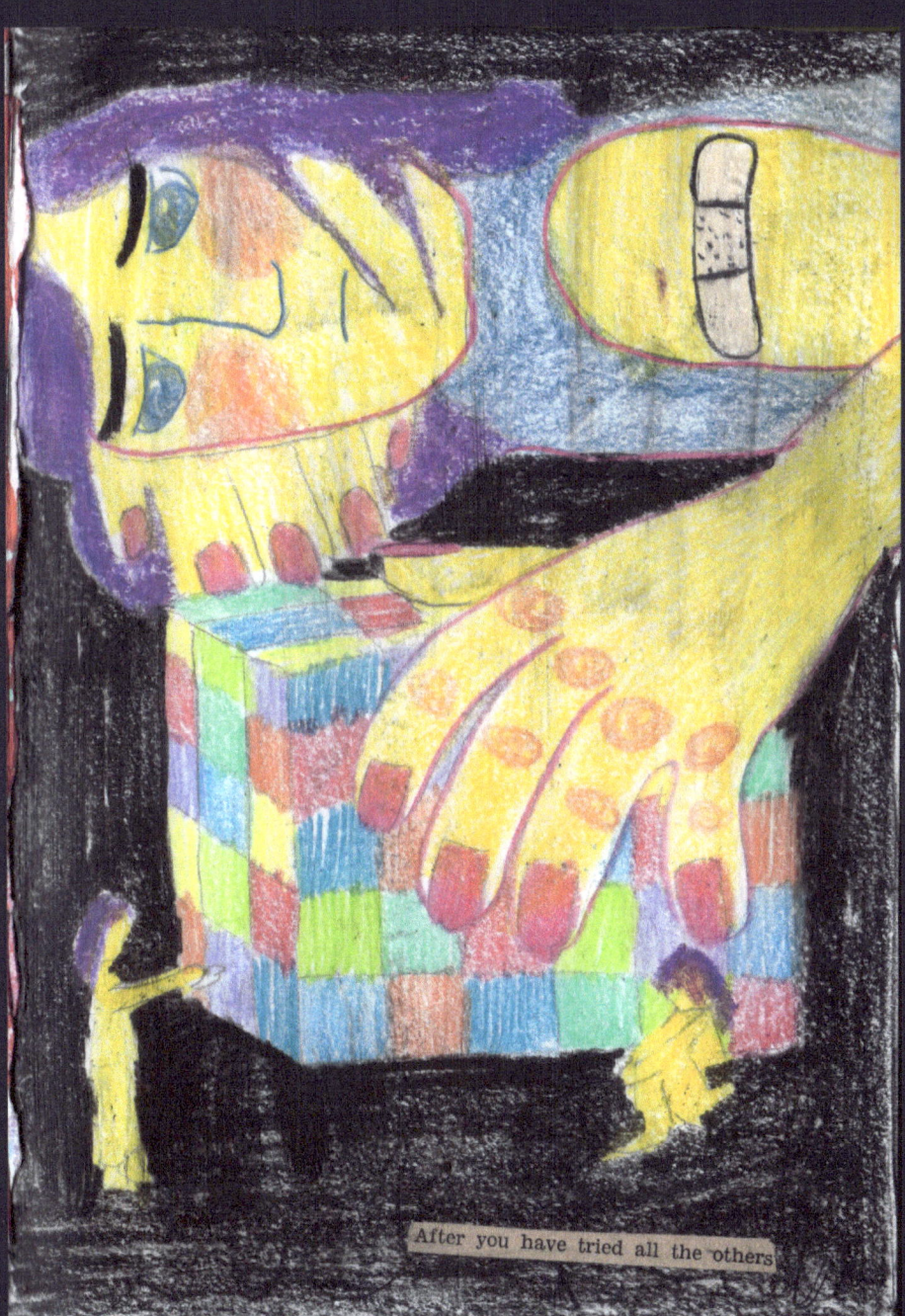

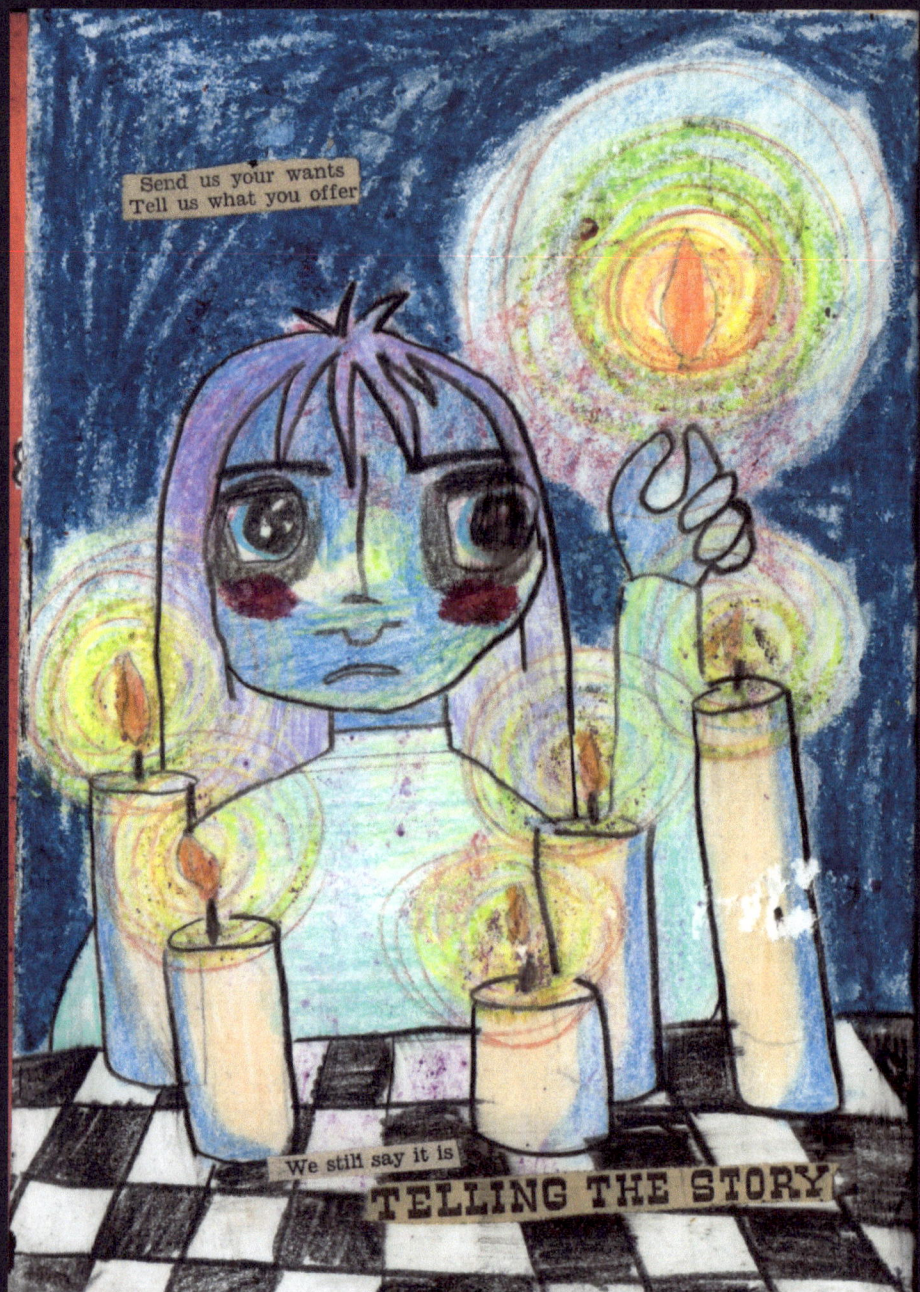

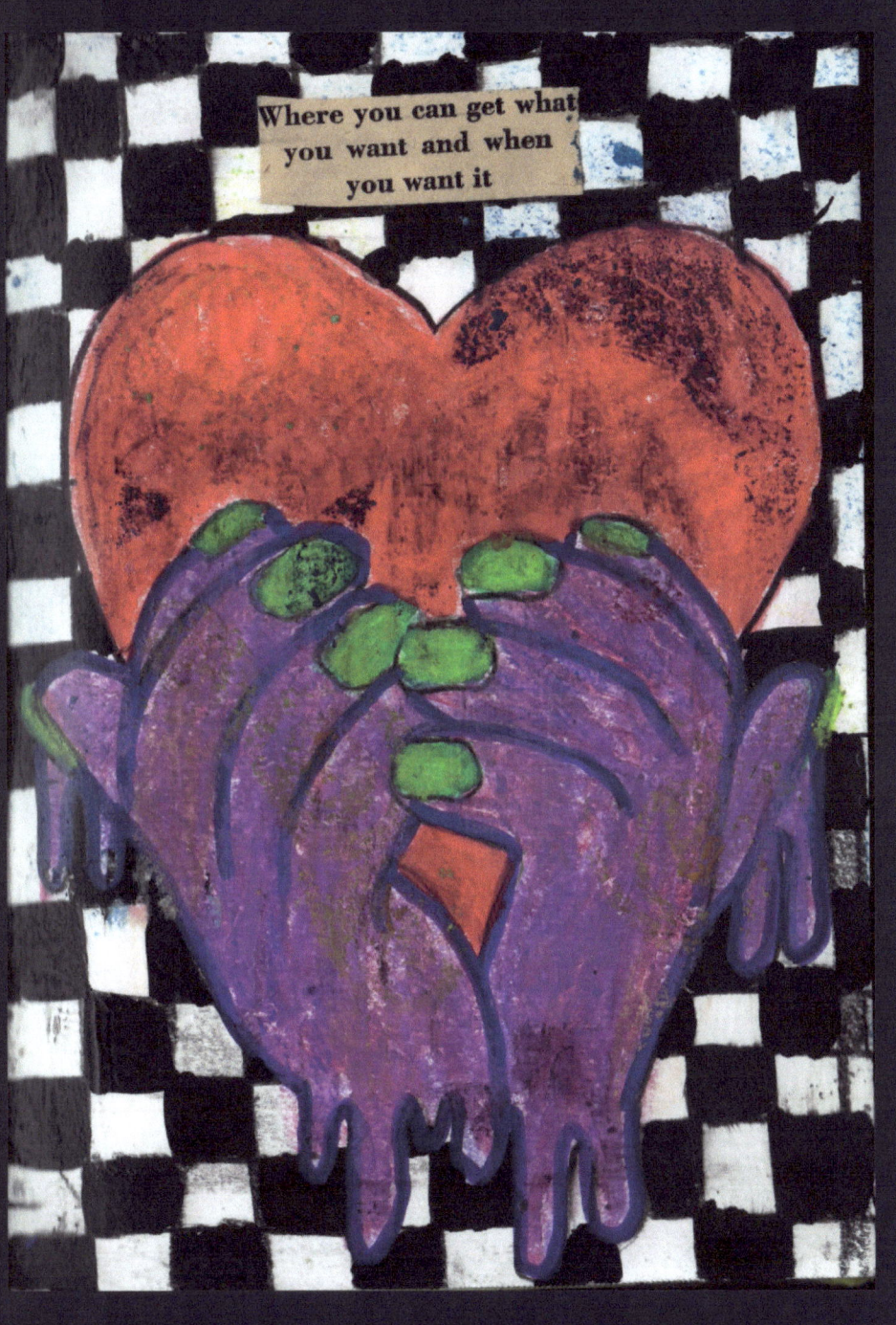

Little can be said about this grand old man that is not already known.

Don't Get Caught!!

Death Valley

The skeleton of a woman
who read the first line
But Refused to read the last.

thank you for your indifference.

www.ingramcontent.com/pod-product-compliance
Lightning Source LLC
Chambersburg PA
CBHW040341220526
45473CB00009B/2760